THE 21 LIFE RULES EVERY CHILD SHOULD LIVE BY

By

Nick Imoru

Achievers Publishing
Calgary, Canada

THE 21 LIFE RULES EVERY CHILD SHOULD LIVE BY

Dedication

To my parents,

For your unwavering love, guidance, and the values you instilled in me, shaping the foundation of my life.

To my school teachers,

At every stage of my education—elementary, junior high, high school, and beyond—thank you for your patience, encouragement, and dedication to my growth and learning. Your lessons extended far beyond the classroom, leaving a lasting impact.

To my spiritual teachers and mentors,

For nurturing my faith, teaching me God's Word, and guiding me on the path of wisdom and purpose. Your influence has been a beacon of light in my life, helping me become who and what I am today.

This book is a reflection of all the love, care, and knowledge I've received from each of you. It is my tribute to the lessons you've taught me and the seeds of wisdom you've planted in my heart.

With deepest gratitude,

Nick Imoru

Table of Contents

Contents

Introduction: A Guide for Every Child

Dear Reader,

Welcome to **"The 21 Life Rules Every Child Should Live By."** This book is written especially for you, with love and care, to help guide you as you grow into a kind, strong, and wise person. Each rule is designed to teach you important lessons about how to live a happy, safe, and meaningful life. These rules are like seeds planted in your heart, meant to help you grow into the amazing person God created you to be.

Why I Wrote This Book

As a parent, I want to give my children the best tools to navigate life. Life can be full of decisions, challenges, and opportunities, and I believe having clear rules can make it easier for them to make the right choices. Here are the reasons behind this book:

1. **A Template of Rules for Teaching and Correction:**

   I want to create a simple and clear guide that I can easily refer to when teaching or correcting my children. Whether it's about being honest, staying safe, or respecting others; these rules provide the foundation for lessons that every child should learn.

2. **A Reference Point for Misbehavior:**

   When my children misbehave or forget what's expected of them, I can ask them to read a specific rule to remind them of the right way to act. This book is not just for reading but also for reflecting and remembering.

3. **A Quick Reminder System:**

   By asking, "Do you remember Rule #6?" or "What does Rule #14 say about following instructions?" I can help them align their actions with the values we've set as a family. This makes correction not just about discipline but also about learning and growing.

4. **A Tablet of Family Values:**

Just like the Ten Commandments God gave to Moses, I want this book to be a guide that my children can keep close as they grow. It's a family reference book filled with wisdom, love, and faith—rules that will guide them in life, no matter where they go.

5. **Our Family Rules:**

These are the rules we follow at home as a family. They're our shared values and principles, shaping the way we treat each other and live together in love and harmony.

6. **A Tool for a Bright Future:**

My hope is that these rules will help my children grow into wonderful, kind, and confident individuals. By following these principles, they will be equipped to face life's challenges and build a great future.

7. **A Training Manual for Life:**

The Bible teaches us in Proverbs 22:6:

"Train up a child in the way he should go; even when he is old he will not depart from it."

This book is a practical tool to help fulfill this verse—a guide to train children in wisdom and righteousness, setting them on the right path.

8. **A Source of Answers:**

   When my children have questions about life—about how to treat others, make decisions, or deal with challenges—I want to have something to refer them to. This book is here to provide those answers, grounded in love, faith, and practical wisdom.

How to Use This Book

This book is more than just a list of rules—it's a guide to help you grow and thrive. Each rule has been carefully written to teach you how to make good choices, treat others with kindness, and stay true to yourself. You can use this book in many ways:

- Read it with your parents or on your own to learn valuable lessons.

- Refer to specific rules when you're unsure about what to do in a situation.

- Remember the rules when your parents remind you of them to help you stay on track.

- Reflect on the Bible verses and lessons included in each rule to grow closer to God.

A Lifelong Gift

As you grow up, you'll face many situations where you'll need to decide what's right and wrong. This book is here to help you make those decisions with confidence and faith. My hope is that these rules will not only guide you today but also stay with you for the rest of your life, helping you become the amazing person God made you to be.

So, let's begin this journey together! Open your heart, learn the lessons, and let these rules guide your steps. Remember, God is always with you, cheering you on as you live by His principles and grow into a shining light in the world.

With love,

Nick Imoru

Rule #1: Obey, Honor, and Always Trust in God

Hi there! Did you know that God loves you so much and wants to be your best friend? He wants you to live a happy and blessed life. To do that, you need to obey Him, honor Him, and always trust Him. Let's talk about how you can do this every day!

Pray Daily

Talking to God is like having a conversation with your best friend. That's what prayer is—talking to God about anything and everything.

- **Why Pray?**

    When you pray, you're letting God know you love Him and trust Him to take care of you. You can thank Him for the good things, ask for help, or even share how you're feeling.

- **What the Bible Says:**

    Jesus prayed a lot! In Mark 1:35, we read:

    "Very early in the morning, while it was still dark, Jesus got up, left the house and went off to a solitary place, where he prayed."

If Jesus made time to pray, we should too!

- **How to Pray:**

    You don't need fancy words. Just say something like:

    "Dear God, thank You for loving me. Please help me to be kind and to do well in school. Amen."

Read the Bible

The Bible is like a treasure map that leads you to God's amazing plan for your life. When you read it, you learn how much He loves you and how He wants you to live.

- **Why Read the Bible?**

    The Bible helps you make good choices. Psalms 119:105 says:

"Your word is a lamp to my feet, a light on my path."

It's like a flashlight for your life!

- **Getting Started:**

Start with Bible stories about people like Noah, David, and Jesus. Ask an adult to read with you if you don't understand something.

Follow God's Teachings

God gave us instructions in the Bible so we can live in a way that makes Him happy and help others too.

- **What God Wants You to Do:**

Jesus said in John 14:15:

"If you love me, keep my commandments."

This means loving others, being honest, and doing what's right.

- **How You Can Do It:**

When you're tempted to do something wrong, like lying or being mean, remember what God says:

"Do not be overcome by evil, but overcome evil with good." (Romans 12:21)

Remember God is With You

Do you ever feel scared or alone? You don't have to, because God is always with you!

- **What the Bible Says:**

  Isaiah 41:10 tells us:

  "So do not fear, for I am with you; do not be dismayed, for I am your God. I will strengthen you and help you."

- **What This Means for You:**

  If you're scared of the dark, about to take a test, or trying something new, remember that God is right there cheering you on.

Pray for Strength

Sometimes life can feel tough, but God will give you the strength to keep going.

- **What the Bible Says:**

  Philippians 4:13 says:

  "I can do all things through Christ who strengthens me."

- **What You Can Do:**

  Say a prayer like this:

  "God, I feel nervous, but I know You're with me. Please help me be brave."

Let's Think About It!

- What can you talk to God about in your prayers?

- How can reading the Bible help you make better choices?

- Can you think of a time when God helped you feel brave?

God loves you and wants you to live your best life! When you pray, read the Bible, follow His teachings, and trust that He's always with you, you'll grow stronger in your faith every day. Keep trusting in Him—He's got you!

Rule #2: Be Kind and Respectful

Hello there! Did you know that being kind and respectful can make the world a happier and more peaceful place? When you treat others with kindness and respect, you show them that they are important and loved. Let's learn how you can be kind and respectful every day!

Treat Others with Kindness

Kindness is like a warm hug for the heart—it makes people feel good and helps them smile. When you choose to be kind, you're doing something God loves.

- **What is Kindness?**

  Being kind means using gentle words, helping others, and showing care. It's as simple as saying "please," "thank you," or helping a friend who's having a bad day.

- **What the Bible Says:**

Ephesians 4:32 says:

"Be kind to one another, tenderhearted, forgiving one another, as God in Christ forgave you."

God wants us to treat others the same way He treats us—with love and kindness.

- **How to Show Kindness:**

Here are some ideas:

- Share your toys or snacks.

- Help a friend with their homework.

- Say something nice to someone who seems sad, like, "You're doing great!"

Respect Adults and Peers

Respect is showing that you value others, whether they're grown-ups or kids like you. It's about listening, being polite, and treating people the way you want to be treated.

- **Respecting Adults:**

Adults, like your parents and teachers, work hard to take care of you and teach you important lessons. Show respect by:

- Listening when they speak.

- Following their instructions.

- Saying "thank you" when they help you.

- **What the Bible Says:**

In Exodus 20:12, the Bible says:

"Honor your father and your mother, so that you may live long in the land the Lord your God is giving you."

Respecting your parents pleases God and brings blessings into your life.

- **Respecting Peers:**

Your friends and classmates also deserve respect. This means:

- Sharing and taking turns.

- Listening when someone is talking.

- - Not teasing or calling people mean names.

- **What Jesus Said:**

  In Matthew 7:12, Jesus teaches:

  "So in everything, do to others what you would have them do to you."

  Think about how you want others to treat you, and do the same for them.

Let's Think About It!

- Can you think of a time when someone was kind to you? How did it make you feel?

- How can you show kindness to someone who is feeling lonely?

- What are some ways you can respect your parents and teachers today?

Kindness and respect are like superpowers—they can make someone's day brighter and help you build strong friendships. Remember, every time you're kind and respectful, you're following God's plan and spreading His love. You've got this!

Rule #3: Be Honest

Hey there! Did you know that honesty is like a golden key that opens the door to trust and good friendships? Being honest means telling the truth and taking responsibility for what you do. Let's explore how you can practice honesty every day and why it's so important!

Tell the Truth

The truth is powerful. It helps people trust you and makes your heart feel light and happy. Even when it's hard, telling the truth is always the right thing to do.

- **Why Is Telling the Truth Important?**

  When you tell the truth, people know they can believe you. It shows that you are trustworthy and strong.

- **What the Bible Says:**

Proverbs 12:22 says:

"The Lord detests lying lips, but he delights in people who are trustworthy." God is happy when you are honest because honesty reflects His goodness.

- **When Should You Tell the Truth?**

    - When someone asks if you've done something wrong, like breaking a toy or forgetting your homework.

    - When you're asked how you feel or what you think.

        Always remember, the truth may be hard to say, but it brings peace and helps you grow.

- **What If You Make a Mistake?**

If you mess up, don't try to cover it up with a lie. Instead, be brave and admit what happened.

Own Your Actions

Taking responsibility for your actions means admitting when you've done something wrong and trying to fix it. It's a big step toward being a strong and trustworthy person.

- **What Does It Mean to Own Your Actions?**

  It means saying, "Yes, I did that," even when it's hard. It's also about learning from your mistakes so you don't repeat them.

- **What the Bible Says:**

  In 1 John 1:9, the Bible says:

  "If we confess our sins, he is faithful and just to forgive us our sins and to cleanse us from all unrighteousness."

  God forgives us when we admit our mistakes, and this helps us become better.

- **How to Take Responsibility:**

  - Say "I'm sorry" if you hurt someone.

- Fix the problem if you can. For example, if you spill milk, clean it up.

- Promise to do better next time and mean it.

- **What If You Don't Take Responsibility?**

  If you blame others or try to hide what you did, it can hurt your friendships and make things worse. Owning up to your actions shows courage and builds trust.

Let's Think About It!

- Can you think of a time when telling the truth made you feel good?

- Why is it important to admit when you've made a mistake?

- How can you make things right if you've hurt someone's feelings?

Being honest means more than just telling the truth—it means living in a way that reflects God's love and goodness. When you're honest and responsible, people will trust and respect you, and you'll feel proud of the person you're becoming. You're doing great—keep it up!

Rule #4: Learn to Forgive

Hi there! Have you ever been hurt by someone and found it hard to let go of the pain? Forgiving others can be tough, but it's one of the most powerful things you can do. When you forgive, you let go of anger and make room for peace in your heart. Let's talk about why forgiveness is important and how you can practice it.

Don't Hold Grudges

Holding onto anger or bad feelings doesn't make things better—it makes your heart feel heavy. When you forgive, you free yourself from those feelings and allow your heart to heal.

- **Why You Shouldn't Hold Grudges:**

  Carrying a grudge is like carrying a backpack full of rocks. It slows you down and makes you feel tired. Forgiving someone is like taking off the backpack—you feel lighter and happier.

- **What the Bible Says:**

Ephesians 4:31-32 teaches us:

"Let all bitterness and wrath and anger and clamor and slander be put away from you, along with all malice. Be kind to one another, tenderhearted, forgiving one another, as God in Christ forgave you."

God wants you to let go of anger and forgive because He has forgiven you.

- **How to Let Go of a Grudge:**
  - Think about how much better you'll feel once you forgive.
  - Pray and ask God to help you let go of your anger.
  - Remember that everyone makes mistakes—even you!

Be Peaceful

Forgiveness brings peace, not just to you but to everyone around you. When you choose peace over anger, you're being a peacemaker, just like Jesus wants you to be.

- **Why Forgiveness Brings Peace:**

  When you forgive, you stop arguments and hurt feelings from growing. It helps repair relationships and makes life more joyful.

- **What the Bible Says:**

  Matthew 5:9 says:

  "Blessed are the peacemakers, for they will be called children of God."

  When you forgive and choose peace, you are following in Jesus' footsteps.

- **How to Be Peaceful:**

  - Speak kindly, even when you're upset.

  - If you have a disagreement, try to understand the other person's side.

- Say, "I forgive you," and mean it.

What About Big Hurts?

Sometimes people hurt us in big ways, and forgiving them feels really hard. Remember, forgiveness doesn't mean saying what they did was okay—it means choosing to let go of the anger so it doesn't hurt you anymore.

- **What the Bible Says:**

  In Colossians 3:13, we're reminded:

  "Bear with each other and forgive one another if any of you has a grievance against someone. Forgive as the Lord forgave you."

  God forgives us even when we make big mistakes, and He helps us forgive others too.

Let's Think About It!

- How do you feel when someone forgives you?

- Why is it important to let go of anger and forgive?

- Who is someone you can forgive today, and how will you do it?

Forgiveness is a gift you give to yourself and others. It clears your heart of anger and makes space for love and peace. The more you practice forgiveness, the happier and freer you'll feel. You've got this!

Rule #5: Be Confident

Hey there! Did you know that God made you special and unique? He gave you amazing talents and abilities, so there's no need to doubt yourself. Being confident means believing in yourself, speaking up, and knowing that you don't have to compare yourself to anyone else. Let's dive in and discover how to be your best, most confident self!

Believe in Yourself

Believing in yourself means knowing that you are valuable, capable, and loved just the way you are. God made you for a purpose, and He is always with you to help you succeed.

- **Why You Should Believe in Yourself:**

  When you believe in yourself, you're more likely to try new things, solve problems, and chase your dreams. It's okay to make mistakes—that's how you learn and grow!

- **What the Bible Says:**

Philippians 4:13 reminds us:

"I can do all things through Christ who strengthens me."

God gives you the strength to do amazing things, so don't be afraid to try.

- **How to Build Confidence:**

  - Remind yourself of things you're good at.

  - Pray and ask God for courage when you feel unsure.

  - Say positive things to yourself, like:

    "I can do this! God is with me."

Speak Up

Your thoughts and ideas are important! Speaking up shows that you believe in yourself and have something valuable to share. Whether it's asking a question, sharing an idea, or standing up for what's right, your voice matters.

- **Why Speaking Up is Important:**

  When you speak up, you can help others understand you and solve problems. Staying silent out of fear might make you miss opportunities to shine.

- **What the Bible Says:**

  In 2 Timothy 1:7, we're told:

  "For the Spirit God gave us does not make us timid, but gives us power, love and self-discipline."

  God has given you the courage to use your voice!

- **How to Speak Up:**

  - Start by practicing with people you trust, like family or close friends.

  - Take a deep breath and speak clearly.

- Remember, even if you feel nervous, you're doing something brave!

Don't Compare Yourself to Others

Have you ever looked at someone and thought they were better than you? Comparing yourself to others can make you feel sad or small, but guess what? You are one of a kind, and that's something to celebrate!

- **Why You Shouldn't Compare Yourself:**

  God made everyone different on purpose. Your talents and strengths are just as important as someone else's.

- **What the Bible Says:**

  In Psalm 139:14, it says:

  "I praise you because I am fearfully and wonderfully made; your works are wonderful, I know that full well."

  God created you wonderfully, so don't worry about being like anyone else.

- **How to Stop Comparing Yourself:**

  - Focus on your own strengths and progress.

  - Celebrate other people's successes without feeling bad about yourself.

  - Thank God for making you unique.

Let's Think About It!

- What is one thing you're really good at?

- When was the last time you spoke up about something important? How did it feel?

- How can you remind yourself not to compare yourself to others?

Confidence is like a bright light inside you that shines when you believe in yourself and trust that God is always there to help you. So stand tall, speak up, and remember—you are wonderfully made! Keep being amazing!

Rule #6: Don't Be Afraid to Say No

Hi there! Have you ever been in a situation where someone asked you to do something you knew wasn't right or made you feel uncomfortable? It's okay to say no! Learning to say no helps you stand up for yourself, set healthy boundaries, and stay true to what's right. Let's talk about how you can do this with confidence and kindness.

Stand Up for Yourself

Standing up for yourself means knowing what's right and being brave enough to say so. It's about protecting yourself from being treated unfairly or doing things you don't feel good about.

- **Why It's Important to Stand Up for Yourself:**

  When you stand up for yourself, you show self-respect and teach others how to treat you. It's not about being rude—it's about being strong and true to yourself.

- **What the Bible Says:**

In Joshua 1:9, God encourages us:

"Have I not commanded you? Be strong and courageous. Do not be afraid; do not be discouraged, for the Lord your God will be with you wherever you go."

God is always with you, giving you the courage to stand up for what's right.

- **How to Stand Up for Yourself:**

  - Say "no" if someone pressures you to do something wrong.

  - Speak clearly and firmly without yelling.

  - Remember, it's okay to walk away from people or situations that don't feel right.

Set Boundaries

Boundaries are like invisible lines that protect you from being hurt or taken advantage of. They help you decide what is okay and what isn't.

- **Why Setting Boundaries is Important:**

  Boundaries teach people how to treat you with respect. They also help you stay safe and happy.

- **What the Bible Says:**

  Proverbs 4:23 says:

  "Above all else, guard your heart, for everything you do flows from it."

  Setting boundaries is one way to guard your heart and protect yourself.

- **How to Set Boundaries:**

  - Decide what you're comfortable with and what you're not.

  - Tell others your limits kindly but firmly. For example, say:

"I don't like it when you yell at me. Please speak kindly."

- Stick to your boundaries, even if others push back.

Be Firm but Polite

Saying no doesn't mean being mean or rude. You can say no in a way that is kind and respectful, while still standing your ground.

- **Why It's Important to Be Firm but Polite:**

  Being polite shows that you respect others, even when you disagree. Being firm shows that you respect yourself and your decisions.

- **What the Bible Says:**

  Colossians 4:6 encourages us:

  "Let your speech always be gracious, seasoned with salt, so that you may know how you ought to answer each person."

Your words can be kind and strong at the same time!

- **How to Be Firm but Polite:**

    - Use calm and respectful words. For example:

        "Thank you, but I don't want to do that."

    - Avoid arguing or yelling—it's okay to simply walk away if someone doesn't listen.

    - Practice what you'll say ahead of time if you think you'll need to say no.

Let's Think About It!

- Can you think of a time when you said no to something that wasn't right? How did it feel?

- What are some boundaries you can set to protect yourself?

- How can you stay polite while being firm when saying no?

Saying no is not selfish—it's a way to take care of yourself and stay true to your values. Remember, God is always with you, helping you to be strong and courageous. You're doing an awesome job—keep it up!

Rule #7: Handle Bullies Wisely

Hey there! Have you ever dealt with someone who was mean or unkind to you or others? That person might be a bully. Bullying can be hurtful, but you don't have to face it alone. God gives you the courage and wisdom to handle bullies the right way—with strength, kindness, and the support of people who care about you. Let's learn how!

Stay Calm and Confident

When a bully tries to upset you, staying calm and confident shows them that their words or actions don't have power over you. It can even stop the situation from getting worse.

- **Why Staying Calm Helps:**

When you don't react with fear or anger, the bully may lose interest in bothering you. Calmness shows strength and self-control.

- **What the Bible Says:**

Proverbs 15:1 reminds us:

"A gentle answer turns away wrath, but a harsh word stirs up anger."

Responding calmly can help avoid making the situation worse.

- **How to Stay Calm:**

  - Take a deep breath and count to five before saying anything.

  - Stand tall and look the bully in the eye.

  - Use a firm voice to say something simple like:

    "I don't like what you're saying. Please stop."

Speak Up to a Trusted Adult

You don't have to deal with bullying on your own. Talking to a parent, teacher, or another adult you trust can help solve the problem and keep you safe.

- **Why Speaking Up is Important:**

  Bullying can make you feel scared or upset, but telling an adult can stop it from continuing. Adults have the tools and authority to step in and help.

- **What the Bible Says:**

  In Psalm 121:2, it says:

  "My help comes from the Lord, the Maker of heaven and earth."

  God often sends help through the people He places in your life, like parents and teachers.

- **How to Speak Up:**

  - Choose an adult you trust, like your mom, dad, teacher, or school counselor.

- Explain what's happening in a clear and calm way. For example:

  "There's someone at school who is being mean to me, and I don't know what to do."

- Ask for advice or help in handling the situation.

Be a Friend to Others

Sometimes, bullies act the way they do because they are hurting or feel lonely. While you should protect yourself, showing kindness can make a difference. Being a friend to others who are being bullied also helps create a safe and loving environment.

- **Why Kindness Matters:**

  Kindness can change hearts, even the heart of a bully. It also makes you a leader who stands up for what is right.

- **What the Bible Says:**

  Romans 12:21 encourages us:

"Do not be overcome by evil, but overcome evil with good."

Responding to unkindness with kindness shows strength and reflects God's love.

- **How to Be a Friend:**

    - Offer to sit with someone who looks sad or lonely.

    - Stand up for a classmate who is being bullied by saying something kind like:

      "Leave them alone. That's not nice."

    - Pray for the bully, asking God to help them change and find peace in their heart.

Let's Think About It!

- How can staying calm help you handle a bully?

- Who are some trusted adults you can talk to if you're being bullied?

- How can you show kindness to someone who seems lonely or upset?

Handling bullies wisely shows courage, kindness, and faith in God's ability to help you. Remember, you are never alone—God is always with you, and so are the people who care about you. Stay strong and keep being a shining light wherever you go!

Rule #8: Treat Others How You Want to Be Treated

Hi there! Do you like it when people are kind to you, include you in games, and treat you with respect? Of course, you do! That's why it's important to treat others the same way. When you treat others how you want to be treated, you make the world a happier and more loving place. Let's learn how to do this every day!

Be Kind, Not Hurtful

Kindness is a choice you make to show love and respect to others. When you are kind, you help people feel happy and valued. Hurtful words or actions can leave scars, so choose kindness instead.

- **Why Kindness Matters:**

Kindness spreads joy and makes people feel good. Even small acts of kindness, like a smile or a kind word, can brighten someone's day.

- **What the Bible Says:**

In Matthew 7:12, Jesus teaches:

"So in everything, do to others what you would have them do to you."

This means treating others with the same love and care you'd like to receive.

- **How to Be Kind:**

  - Say nice things, like "Thank you" or "You did a great job!"

  - Help someone in need, like picking up something they dropped.

  - Avoid saying or doing anything that might hurt someone's feelings.

Include Everyone

Imagine being left out of a game or activity—it doesn't feel good, does it? Including everyone makes people feel welcome and valued. It's a way to show love and kindness.

- **Why Including Others is Important:**

  When you include others, you're showing them that they matter. You're also making new friends and creating a sense of belonging.

- **What the Bible Says:**

  Romans 15:7 says:

  "Accept one another, then, just as Christ accepted you, in order to bring praise to God."

  Including others shows God's love and makes Him happy.

- **How to Include Everyone:**

  - Invite someone who looks left out to join your game.

  - Ask someone sitting alone to sit with you.

- Be friendly to new classmates or neighbors, even if they seem different from you.

What If Someone is Unkind to You?

Even if someone isn't kind to you, you can still choose to treat them with kindness. This doesn't mean letting them be mean to you, but it does mean showing them love instead of anger.

- **What the Bible Says:**

  Luke 6:31 reminds us:

  "Do to others as you would have them do to you."

  Your kindness can inspire others to change their ways and treat people better.

Let's Think About It!

- How do you feel when someone is kind to you?

- Why is it important to include everyone, even if they are different from you?

- Can you think of one person you can include in something today?

Treating others how you want to be treated is a powerful way to show love, kindness, and respect. Remember, your actions can make a big difference in someone's life, so choose to be kind and include everyone. Keep spreading God's love everywhere you go!

Rule #9: Stay Curious and Open-Minded

Hi there! Did you know that being curious and open-minded helps you grow, learn, and discover amazing things? God created a big, beautiful world full of exciting lessons, new ideas, and incredible opportunities. Staying curious means always wanting to learn, and being open-minded means being willing to try new things and listen to others. Let's explore how you can develop a growth mindset!

Ask Questions

Asking questions is how you learn and grow. It's okay to not know everything—being curious means you're eager to find out more.

- **Why Asking Questions is Important:**

Questions help you discover new things about the world, other people, and even yourself. They also show that you're paying attention and want to understand.

- **What the Bible Says:**

Proverbs 18:15 says:

"The heart of the discerning acquires knowledge, for the ears of the wise seek it out."

God encourages us to ask questions and seek knowledge because it helps us grow wise.

- **How to Ask Questions:**

  - If you don't understand something, say, "Can you explain that to me?"

  - Be curious about God's Word and ask questions about the Bible.

  - Don't be afraid to ask, "Why?"—it's how great discoveries start!

Be Willing to Learn

Learning doesn't stop at school—it's something you can do every day. Being willing to learn means listening to others, reading books, and being open to new ideas.

- **Why Learning is Important:**

  Learning helps you grow your skills, understand the world better, and make good decisions. It also helps you become the person God wants you to be.

- **What the Bible Says:**

  Proverbs 9:9 says:

  "Instruct the wise and they will be wiser still; teach the righteous and they will add to their learning."

  God wants us to keep learning so we can grow in wisdom.

- **How to Be Willing to Learn:**

  - Listen when others share their ideas, even if they're different from yours.

- Try to learn something new every day, like a fun fact, a skill, or a Bible verse.

- Ask God to help you learn and understand things better.

Try New Things

Trying new things can be exciting and a little scary at the same time, but it's how you grow and discover your talents and interests.

- **Why Trying New Things is Important:**

  When you try new things, you learn what you're good at and what you enjoy. It also helps you become more confident and brave.

- **What the Bible Says:**

  Isaiah 43:19 says:

  "See, I am doing a new thing! Now it springs up; do you not perceive it?"

God loves doing new things in our lives, and He encourages us to step into the unknown with faith.

- **How to Try New Things:**

    - Join a new activity at school or church.

    - Taste a new food you've never tried before.

    - Take on a challenge, like learning to ride a bike or trying out for a team.

Let's Think About It!

- What's something you're curious about and would like to learn more about?

- Can you think of a question you'd like to ask about the Bible or the world?

- What's one new thing you can try this week?

Staying curious and open-minded helps you grow into the amazing person God created you to be. Don't be afraid to ask questions, learn from others, and try new things. You'll discover so much about God's world, other people, and even yourself. Keep exploring and growing—you're doing great!

Rule #10: Dream Big

Hey there! Did you know that God has amazing plans for your life? He wants you to dream big and believe in the incredible possibilities He can bring into your life. When you set goals and trust in Him, there's no limit to what you can achieve. Let's talk about how you can dream big, set goals, and believe in the wonderful future God has for you!

Set Goals

A goal is like a map—it shows you where you want to go and helps you figure out how to get there. Setting goals gives your dreams direction and helps you stay focused.

- **Why Setting Goals is Important:**

  Goals help you work toward something exciting. They remind you to keep trying, even when things feel hard. Each small step you take brings you closer to your dream.

- **What the Bible Says:**

In Habakkuk 2:2, God says:

"Write down the revelation and make it plain on tablets so that a herald may run with it."

This reminds us to write down our goals and take steps toward achieving them.

- **How to Set Goals:**

  - Think about something you want to achieve, like learning a new skill or doing better in school.

  - Write it down and break it into smaller steps. For example, if your goal is to read a book, start with one chapter at a time.

  - Pray and ask God to guide you as you work on your goals.

Believe in Possibilities

Believing in possibilities means trusting that great things can happen when you work hard and have faith in God. Even if something seems impossible, remember that with God, anything is possible!

- **Why Believing in Possibilities is Important:**

  When you believe in possibilities, you're more willing to try new things, face challenges, and keep going even when it's tough. It helps you stay positive and hopeful.

- **What the Bible Says:**

  In Matthew 19:26, Jesus says:

  "With man this is impossible, but with God all things are possible."

  No dream is too big when God is on your side!

- **How to Believe in Possibilities:**

  - Remind yourself of times when you achieved something you thought was hard.

- Surround yourself with people who encourage you and believe in your dreams.

- Pray and trust God to help you make your dreams come true.

What to Do When Things Feel Hard

Sometimes, you might feel like giving up on your dreams. But don't forget—God is with you, cheering you on!

- **What the Bible Says:**

  In Jeremiah 29:11, God promises:

  "For I know the plans I have for you," declares the Lord, "plans to prosper you and not to harm you, plans to give you hope and a future."

  Trust that God's plans for you are good, and keep moving forward.

- **How to Keep Going:**

  - Take a break, but don't quit.

- Pray for strength and guidance when you feel unsure.

- Celebrate small victories along the way—they're steps toward your big dream!

Let's Think About It!

- What is one big dream you have for your future?

- What small steps can you take today to get closer to your goal?

- How does trusting in God help you believe in big possibilities?

Dreaming big is part of God's plan for you. He wants you to dream, set goals, and believe in all the amazing things you can do with His help. So go ahead—dream big, work hard, and trust that God will guide you every step of the way. You've got this!

Rule #11: Be Patient

Hello! Have you ever wanted something to happen right away, like getting your favorite snack or taking a turn on the playground? It can be hard to wait, but being patient is one of the best ways to show kindness, self-control, and trust in God's perfect timing. Let's talk about why patience is important and how you can practice it every day!

Wait Your Turn

Waiting your turn shows respect for others and helps things run smoothly. Whether you're waiting in line or for your turn to speak, being patient shows that you care about fairness and kindness.

- **Why Waiting Your Turn is Important:**

  When you wait your turn, you're showing respect for others and allowing everyone to have a fair chance. It also helps avoid arguments and confusion.

- **What the Bible Says:**

In Ecclesiastes 3:1, it says:

"There is a time for everything, and a season for every activity under the heavens." This reminds us that everything has its proper time, including waiting our turn.

- **How to Wait Your Turn:**

  - Take deep breaths while you wait to help you stay calm.

  - Think about how others feel when it's their turn—it's their moment to shine.

  - Use the waiting time to think of something nice to say or do when it's your turn.

Don't Rush

Sometimes, when we rush, we make mistakes or miss out on the joy of what we're doing. Taking your time helps you do things better and enjoy the moment.

- **Why You Shouldn't Rush:**

  Rushing can lead to accidents, misunderstandings, or missing out on important details. Patience helps you slow down and do things with care.

- **What the Bible Says:**

  In Proverbs 21:5, it says:

  "The plans of the diligent lead to profit as surely as haste leads to poverty."

  This means that taking your time and being patient leads to better results than rushing through things.

- **How to Avoid Rushing:**

  - Start tasks early so you don't have to hurry.

- Focus on one thing at a time instead of trying to do everything at once.

- Remember that good things take time to grow, just like a plant or a tree.

Trusting God While You Wait

Being patient is also about trusting God's timing. Sometimes we want things to happen quickly, but God knows the best time for everything.

- **What the Bible Says:**

  Psalm 27:14 encourages us:

  "Wait for the Lord; be strong and take heart and wait for the Lord."

  Trusting God while you wait shows faith and helps you grow stronger.

Let's Think About It!

- Can you think of a time when you had to wait for something? How did it feel?

- Why is it important to wait your turn instead of rushing ahead?

- How can you remind yourself to trust God when you feel impatient?

Patience is a superpower that helps you stay calm, be kind, and trust in God's perfect timing. The more you practice patience, the more peaceful and joyful you'll feel. So take your time, wait your turn, and enjoy every step of the journey. You're doing amazing!

Rule #12: Stay Strong and Persevere

Hi there! Life can sometimes feel challenging, but did you know that God gives you the strength to keep going? Staying strong and persevering means not giving up, staying positive, and being brave no matter what comes your way. Let's talk about how you can keep pushing forward with God's help!

Don't Give Up

Sometimes, things can feel really hard—like learning a new skill or solving a tough problem. But when you don't give up, you discover how strong and capable you really are.

- **Why You Shouldn't Give Up:**

  Giving up stops you from reaching your goals, but staying determined helps you grow and succeed. Every time you keep trying, you're one step closer to achieving your dreams.

- **What the Bible Says:**

Galatians 6:9 reminds us:

"Let us not become weary in doing good, for at the proper time we will reap a harvest if we do not give up."

This means your hard work will pay off if you keep going!

- **How to Keep Trying:**

  - Break big tasks into smaller steps so they don't feel overwhelming.

  - Ask for help when you need it—there's no shame in getting support!

  - Remember, every effort you make brings you closer to success.

Stay Positive

Staying positive means focusing on the good things, even when things don't go your way. A positive attitude helps you face challenges with a smile.

- **Why Staying Positive is Important:**

  A positive attitude gives you hope and strength to keep going. It also encourages the people around you to stay strong too.

- **What the Bible Says:**

  In Philippians 4:8, Paul says:

  "Finally, brothers and sisters, whatever is true, whatever is noble, whatever is right, whatever is pure, whatever is lovely, whatever is admirable— if anything is excellent or praiseworthy—think about such things."

  This verse reminds us to focus on the good things God has placed in our lives.

- **How to Stay Positive:**

- Think about what you're thankful for, even when things feel tough.

- Say encouraging things to yourself, like:

  "I can do this! God is with me."

- Surround yourself with people who lift you up and cheer you on.

Be Brave

Being brave doesn't mean you're never afraid—it means you face your fears and challenges with courage and trust in God.

- **Why Being Brave is Important:**

Bravery helps you try new things, face tough situations, and keep going even when you're scared. It's about trusting that God will guide and protect you.

- **What the Bible Says:**

Joshua 1:9 tells us:

"Have I not commanded you? Be strong and courageous. Do not be afraid; do not be discouraged, for the Lord your God will be with you wherever you go."

God promises to be with you, so you don't have to be afraid.

- **How to Be Brave:**

    - Pray and ask God for courage when you feel scared.

    - Take small steps toward facing your fears.

    - Remember that God is with you, cheering you on every step of the way!

Let's Think About It!

- Can you think of a time when you didn't give up? How did it feel when you succeeded?

- What are some ways you can stay positive when things are tough?

- What's something you can be brave about this week?

Staying strong and persevering means trusting God to help you through every challenge. Remember, you are braver, stronger, and more capable than you think. With God by your side, you can achieve great things. Keep going—you've got this!

Rule #13: Take Responsibility

Hello! Did you know that taking responsibility shows that you're growing up and becoming someone people can trust? Being responsible means doing what you're supposed to do, cleaning up after yourself, and always doing your best. Let's talk about how you can take responsibility in everything you do!

Clean Up After Yourself

When you clean up after yourself, you're showing respect for others and your surroundings. Whether it's picking up your toys or tidying your room, taking responsibility for your mess is an important habit.

- **Why Cleaning Up Matters:**

  Cleaning up helps keep your home and school neat and pleasant for everyone. It also shows that you care about your environment.

- **What the Bible Says:**

  In 1 Corinthians 14:40, it says:

  "But everything should be done in a fitting and orderly way."

  Keeping things tidy reflects God's desire for order and care in all things.

- **How to Clean Up After Yourself:**

  - Put your toys away after playing.

  - Clean your dishes after meals or help with the dishes.

  - Keep your room tidy by putting things back where they belong.

Do Your Best in School and Chores

Doing your best shows that you care about the work you do. Whether it's studying for a test or helping out at home, putting in your best effort is part of being responsible.

- **Why Doing Your Best is Important:**

When you give your best effort, you're showing pride in your work and respect for the people counting on you. It also helps you learn and grow.

- **What the Bible Says:**

Colossians 3:23 encourages us:

"Whatever you do, work at it with all your heart, as working for the Lord, not for human masters."

This means doing your best is a way to honor God.

- **How to Do Your Best:**

  - At school: Listen to your teacher, complete your homework, and ask questions if you need help.

  - At home: Help with chores like sweeping, taking out the trash, or setting the table.

  - In everything: Always give your best effort, even when it feels hard.

What Happens When You Take Responsibility?

When you take responsibility, people will trust and respect you. You also feel proud of yourself because you know you've done your part.

- **What the Bible Says:**

  Luke 16:10 teaches us:

  "Whoever can be trusted with very little can also be trusted with much."

  Being responsible with small tasks prepares you for bigger opportunities in the future.

- **How to Handle Mistakes:**

  - If you make a mistake, admit it and try to fix it.

  - Learn from your mistakes so you can do better next time.

  - Remember, being responsible also means asking for forgiveness when necessary.

Let's Think About It!

- How do you feel when you clean up after yourself and see a neat and tidy space?

- What are some chores or school tasks where you can try your best this week?

- Why is it important to take responsibility for your actions?

Taking responsibility helps you grow into someone who is dependable and trustworthy. Whether it's cleaning up, doing your best, or owning up to your mistakes, responsibility shows that you care. Keep practicing—you're on the right track!

Rule #14: Follow Instructions

Hi there! Have you ever been told to do something, like finish your homework or help with chores? Following instructions shows that you respect and value the people who care for you, like your parents, teachers, and elders. It also helps you learn and grow. Let's explore how to follow instructions and why it's so important!

Respect Parents, Teachers, and Elders

Respecting the people who guide and care for you is one of the best ways to show that you appreciate them. When you listen and follow their instructions, you're honoring their wisdom and the role God has given them in your life.

- **Why Respecting Adults is Important:**

Your parents, teachers, and elders want the best for you. Respecting them helps you learn important lessons and keeps you safe.

- **What the Bible Says:**

In Exodus 20:12, God commands:

"Honor your father and your mother, so that you may live long in the land the Lord your God is giving you."

Respecting your parents is one way to honor God.

- **How to Show Respect:**

  - Listen carefully when they talk to you.

  - Do what they ask without complaining.

  - Use polite words like "please" and "thank you."

Be a Good Listener

Good listening is the first step to following instructions. When you listen carefully, you understand what's being asked of you and can do it well.

- **Why Listening is Important:**

  Listening shows that you care about what others are saying. It also helps you avoid mistakes and learn new things.

- **What the Bible Says:**

  In Proverbs 1:5, it says:

  "Let the wise listen and add to their learning, and let the discerning get guidance." Listening helps you grow wiser and make better choices.

- **How to Be a Good Listener:**

    - Look at the person speaking to you so they know you're paying attention.

- Repeat their instructions in your own words to make sure you understand. For example, say:

  "So you want me to clean my room and put my toys away, right?"

- Ask questions if you're not sure about something.

What Happens When You Follow Instructions?

When you follow instructions, things go more smoothly, and people trust you more. You also avoid getting into trouble and learn new skills.

- **What the Bible Says:**

  In Proverbs 13:1, it says:

  "A wise son heeds his father's instruction, but a mocker does not respond to rebukes."

  Listening to guidance shows wisdom and helps you grow into a responsible person.

Let's Think About It!

- Can you think of a time when you followed instructions and things went well?

- Why is it important to respect and listen to your parents and teachers?

- How can you be a better listener when someone is talking to you?

Following instructions is a simple but powerful way to show respect and learn valuable lessons. By listening carefully and doing what's asked of you, you're honoring God and the people who care for you. Keep practicing—you're doing great!

Rule #15: Obey Rules and Be Disciplined

Hi there! Have you ever wondered why we have rules? Rules are like guideposts—they help us stay safe, make good choices, and live peacefully with others. Being disciplined means following these rules and doing what's right, even when it's hard. Let's learn how obeying rules and being disciplined can help you grow into the amazing person God wants you to be!

Follow Family and School Rules

Rules at home and school are there to keep you safe and help you learn. When you follow them, you show respect for those who care for you and make life better for everyone.

- **Why Rules Are Important:**

Rules teach you how to act responsibly and treat others with respect. They also keep you out of trouble and help you succeed in life.

- **What the Bible Says:**

Romans 13:1 reminds us:

"Let everyone be subject to the governing authorities, for there is no authority except that which God has established."

Obeying rules shows that you respect the authority God has placed in your life.

- **Examples of Rules to Follow:**

  - At home: Clean your room, finish your homework, and help with chores.

  - At school: Listen to your teacher, raise your hand to speak, and be kind to your classmates.

  - Anywhere: Follow safety rules like not running in hallways or crossing streets carefully.

Be on Time and Do Your Work

Being disciplined means managing your time well and completing your tasks. It shows that you are dependable and take responsibility for your actions.

- **Why Being On Time is Important:**

  Being on time shows respect for others and helps things run smoothly. It also helps you avoid feeling rushed or stressed.

- **What the Bible Says:**

  In Ecclesiastes 3:1, it says:

  "There is a time for everything, and a season for every activity under the heavens." Being punctual and disciplined helps you use your time wisely.

- **Why Doing Your Work Matters:**

  Completing your tasks, whether it's schoolwork or chores, shows that you are hardworking and reliable. It also makes you feel proud of yourself for doing a good job.

- **How to Be Disciplined:**

    - Set a schedule to manage your time for school, play, and rest.

    - Focus on one task at a time and finish it before moving on to the next.

    - Take breaks when needed, but make sure to get back to work and finish what you started.

What Happens When You Obey Rules and Stay Disciplined?

When you follow rules and stay disciplined, people trust and respect you more. You also feel confident and prepared for bigger responsibilities.

- **What the Bible Says:**

    In Proverbs 10:17, it says:

    "Whoever heeds discipline shows the way to life, but whoever ignores correction leads others astray."

Discipline helps you grow into a wise and responsible person.

Let's Think About It!

- Why do you think rules are important at home and school?

- How can you remind yourself to be on time and finish your work?

- What is one area where you can practice being more disciplined this week?

Obeying rules and being disciplined may not always be easy, but they help you grow into a strong, responsible, and trustworthy person. Remember, God is proud of you when you make good choices and stay on the right path. Keep it up—you're doing great!

Rule #16: Keep Promises

Hi there! Have you ever made a promise to someone? Promises are special because they show people they can count on you. Keeping your promises means sticking to your word and being someone others can trust. Let's learn how to be trustworthy and why keeping promises is so important!

Stick to Your Word

When you make a promise, it's like giving someone your word. Sticking to your word means following through on what you said you would do, even when it's hard.

- **Why Sticking to Your Word is Important:**

  When you keep your promises, people know they can rely on you. It shows that you're honest and dependable.

- **What the Bible Says:**

  In Ecclesiastes 5:4-5, it says:

  "When you make a vow to God, do not delay to fulfill it. He has no pleasure in fools; fulfill your vow. It is better not to make a vow than to make one and not fulfill it."

  This reminds us to think carefully before making promises and to always follow through.

- **How to Stick to Your Word:**

  - Only promise what you know you can do.

  - Write down your promise if it helps you remember.

  - If something unexpected happens, explain and do your best to make it right.

Be Trustworthy

Being trustworthy means people can believe in you and depend on you. It's about being honest, reliable, and someone others feel safe with.

- **Why Being Trustworthy is Important:**

When people trust you, they feel secure and valued. Trust builds strong friendships and relationships.

- **What the Bible Says:**

Proverbs 11:3 says:

"The integrity of the upright guides them, but the unfaithful are destroyed by their duplicity."

Integrity—doing what's right even when no one is watching—makes you trustworthy.

- **How to Be Trustworthy:**

  - Always tell the truth, even when it's hard.

  - Follow through on your commitments, like finishing your homework or helping with chores.

  - Keep private things private if someone trusts you with a secret, unless it's something harmful that an adult needs to know.

What Happens When You Keep Promises?

When you keep promises, people know they can count on you. It also makes you feel good inside because you've done the right thing.

- **What the Bible Says:**

  In Matthew 5:37, Jesus teaches:

  "Let your 'Yes' be 'Yes,' and your 'No,' 'No'; anything beyond this comes from the evil one."

  This verse reminds us to be clear, honest, and dependable in what we say and do.

Let's Think About It!

- Can you think of a promise you've made and kept? How did it feel?

- Why is it important to think before making a promise?

- What can you do to show others that you're trustworthy?

Keeping promises shows that you care about others and value their trust. It helps you build strong relationships and grow into someone people can rely on. Always remember—when you keep your word, you honor God and reflect His faithfulness. Keep being dependable—you're doing a wonderful

Rule #17: Be Grateful

Hello! Have you ever noticed how happy you feel when someone says "thank you" or appreciates something you've done? Being grateful is all about saying "thank you" and valuing the things and people in your life. Gratitude helps you see the good things God has given you and makes your heart feel full. Let's learn how to be grateful every day!

Say Thank You

Saying "thank you" is a simple but powerful way to show gratitude. It tells others that you appreciate what they've done for you or given to you.

- **Why Saying Thank You is Important:**

   Gratitude makes people feel loved and valued. It also reminds you to focus on the blessings in your life instead of what you don't have.

- **What the Bible Says:**

In 1 Thessalonians 5:18, it says:

"Give thanks in all circumstances; for this is God's will for you in Christ Jesus."

God wants us to be thankful, no matter what happens, because it helps us trust Him more.

- **How to Say Thank You:**

  - Say "thank you" to your parents, teachers, and friends when they help you.

  - Thank God in your prayers for His blessings. For example:

    "Thank You, God, for my family, my food, and my home."

  - Write a note or draw a picture to show your appreciation to someone special.

Value What You Have

Being grateful also means cherishing the things and people God has given you. Instead of focusing on what you don't have, learn to appreciate and take care of what you do have.

- **Why Valuing What You Have is Important:**

  When you value what you have, you feel more content and joyful. It also helps you use your blessings wisely and share them with others.

- **What the Bible Says:**

  In Philippians 4:11-12, Paul says:

  "I have learned to be content whatever the circumstances. I know what it is to be in need, and I know what it is to have plenty. I have learned the secret of being content in any and every situation."

  This reminds us to be happy and thankful for what we have, no matter how big or small.

- **How to Value What You Have:**

  - Take care of your belongings, like your toys, books, and clothes.

- Spend time with your family and friends, showing them how much they mean to you.

- Remember that even the little things, like a sunny day or a hug, are blessings from God.

What Happens When You're Grateful?

When you're grateful, you feel happier and more connected to others. Gratitude also helps you trust God more because you see how much He's already done for you.

- **What the Bible Says:**

  Psalm 100:4 encourages us:

  "Enter his gates with thanksgiving and his courts with praise; give thanks to him and praise his name."

  Gratitude brings us closer to God and fills our hearts with joy.

Let's Think About It!

- Who are some people you can thank today, and how will you show your gratitude?

- What are three things you're grateful for right now?

- How can you take better care of the blessings God has given you?

Being grateful makes life brighter and reminds you of how much God loves you. So don't forget to say "thank you" and cherish the blessings you have—you'll feel happier, and others will feel loved too. Keep practicing gratitude every day—you're doing great!

Rule #18: Respect Nature and the World Around You

Hi there! Did you know that God created the whole world for us to enjoy and take care of? From the animals to the trees, rivers, and mountains, everything in nature is a gift from God. Respecting nature means being gentle with animals and protecting the environment so it stays beautiful for everyone. Let's learn how you can do your part to care for God's creation!

Be Gentle with Animals

Animals are part of God's creation, and He wants us to treat them with love and care. Whether it's a pet at home, a bird in the sky, or a butterfly in the garden, being gentle with animals shows kindness and respect for their lives.

- **Why Being Gentle with Animals is Important:**

Animals are living creatures with feelings. Treating them kindly helps them feel safe and cared for. It also shows that you value God's creation.

- **What the Bible Says:**

In Proverbs 12:10, it says:

"The righteous care for the needs of their animals, but the kindest acts of the wicked are cruel."

This verse reminds us to care for animals with kindness and love.

- **How to Be Gentle with Animals:**

  - Handle pets carefully and never hurt them.

  - Don't chase or scare wild animals like birds or squirrels.

  - Feed and care for pets responsibly by giving them food, water, and love.

Protect the Environment

The earth is our home, and God has trusted us to take care of it. Protecting the environment means keeping it clean and safe for everyone—humans, animals, and plants.

- **Why Protecting the Environment is Important:**

  Littering, wasting water, or polluting the air hurts the planet. When you take care of the earth, you're helping future generations enjoy its beauty too.

- **What the Bible Says:**

  In Genesis 2:15, it says:

  "The Lord God took the man and put him in the Garden of Eden to work it and take care of it."

  God gave us the responsibility to look after the earth, just like Adam cared for the Garden of Eden.

- **How to Protect the Environment:**

  - Don't litter—always throw trash in the bin.

  - Recycle paper, plastic, and cans to reduce waste.

  - Save water by turning off the tap when you're not using it.

  - Plant a tree or flowers to make the earth greener and more beautiful.

What Happens When You Respect Nature?

When you respect nature, you help keep the world clean, safe, and beautiful. You also honor God by taking care of the gifts He has given us.

- **What the Bible Says:**

Psalm 24:1 reminds us:

"The earth is the Lord's, and everything in it, the world, and all who live in it."

The world belongs to God, and respecting it shows our love for Him.

Let's Think About It!

- How can you show kindness to animals this week?

- What are some ways you can help protect the environment in your home or school?

- Why do you think God wants us to take care of the earth?

Respecting nature and the world around you are important ways to honor God and show love for His creation. So be gentle with animals, protect the environment, and enjoy the beauty of the world God has made. You're doing an amazing job—keep it up!

Rule #19: Be Safe

Hi there! Staying safe is one of the most important ways to care for yourself and others. When you follow safety rules and take care of your body, you're protecting the special life God gave you. Let's talk about how to stay safe and why it's so important to take good care of yourself!

Follow Safety Rules

Safety rules are there to protect you from getting hurt and to help keep everyone safe. Whether you're at home, school, or outside, following safety rules is an important way to show that you value your life and that of others.

- **Why Following Safety Rules is Important:**

  Safety rules help prevent accidents and keep you out of danger. By following them, you're showing that you're responsible and care about your well-being.

- **What the Bible Says:**

Proverbs 27:12 says:

"The prudent see danger and take refuge, but the simple keep going and pay the penalty."

This reminds us to pay attention to rules and avoid situations that might harm us.

- **Examples of Some Safety Rules to Follow:**

    - Look both ways before crossing the street.

    - Always wear your seatbelt in the car.

    - Follow rules at school, like walking (not running) in the hallways.

    - Never talk to strangers or go anywhere without letting an adult know.

Take Care of Your Body

Your body is a gift from God, and taking care of it helps you stay strong, healthy, and full of energy. Caring for your body includes eating nutritious food, exercising, staying clean, and getting enough rest.

- **Why Taking Care of Your Body is Important:**

   When you take care of your body, you feel better and can do all the things you enjoy. It also honors God, who made you in His image.

- **What the Bible Says:**

   In 1 Corinthians 6:19-20, it says:

   "Do you not know that your bodies are temples of the Holy Spirit, who is in you, whom you have received from God? You are not your own; you were bought at a price. Therefore honor God with your bodies."

   Taking care of your body is a way to thank God for the gift of life.

- **How to Take Care of Your Body:**

  - Eat healthy foods like fruits, vegetables, and whole grains.

  - Drink plenty of water to stay hydrated.

  - Exercise by running, playing, or dancing to keep your body strong.

  - Get enough sleep every night so your body can rest and grow.

What Happens When You Stay Safe?

When you follow safety rules and take care of your body, you feel better, avoid getting hurt, and are able to enjoy life to the fullest. You also show God that you're grateful for the body He gave you.

- **What the Bible Says:**

Psalm 121:7-8 promises:

"The Lord will keep you from all harm—he will watch over your life; the Lord will watch over your coming and going both now and forevermore."

God watches over you, and He wants you to stay safe and healthy.

Let's Think About It!

- What are some safety rules you can follow every day to stay safe?

- How can you take better care of your body this week?

- Why do you think God wants you to protect yourself and stay healthy?

Being safe and taking care of your body are important ways to live a happy, healthy life. By following safety rules and looking after yourself, you're showing love and respect for the wonderful gift of life God has given you. Keep up the great work—you're doing amazing!

Rule #20: Use Your Time Wisely

Hi there! Did you know that the way you use your time shapes how much you can learn, grow, and have fun? God gives each of us the same amount of time every day, and it's up to us to use it wisely. By balancing work and play and limiting screen time, you can make the most of every moment. Let's learn how!

Balance Play and Work

Work and play are both important, but they need to be balanced. Work helps you learn and grow, while play helps you relax and enjoy life. When you find the right balance, you can do well in school, help out at home, and still have time for fun.

- **Why Balancing Play and Work is Important:**

  If you play too much, you might not finish your homework or chores. If you work too much, you might feel tired and stressed. Balancing both keeps your life happy and healthy.

- **What the Bible Says:**

In Ecclesiastes 3:1, it says:

"There is a time for everything, and a season for every activity under the heavens." God wants us to use our time wisely, giving the right amount to work, play, and rest.

- **How to Balance Play and Work:**

  - Do your homework or chores first, then reward yourself with playtime.

  - Set a schedule to make sure you have time for everything.

  - Make work fun by turning it into a game or challenge, like racing to finish your chores.

Limit Screen Time

Screens like TVs, tablets, and phones can be fun, but too much screen time can take away from important things like spending time with family, playing outside, or studying. Limiting screen time helps you stay healthy and connected with the world around you.

- **Why Limiting Screen Time is Important:**

  Too much screen time can make you feel tired, take away from real-life fun, and even affect your health. By limiting it, you have more time for creative activities and building relationships.

- **What the Bible Says:**

  In Psalm 90:12, it says:

  "Teach us to number our days, that we may gain a heart of wisdom."

  This reminds us to use our time wisely and focus on what truly matters.

- **How to Limit Screen Time:**

  - Set a timer to remind you when it's time to turn off the screen.

  - Spend time reading, drawing, or playing outside instead.

  - Use screens for learning and creativity, not just for games or videos.

What Happens When You Use Your Time Wisely?

When you balance work and play and limit screen time, you feel happier, healthier, and more productive. You also have more time for the things that truly matter, like spending time with family, helping others, and growing closer to God.

- **What the Bible Says:**

In Colossians 4:5, it says:

"Be wise in the way you act toward outsiders; make the most of every opportunity."

Using your time wisely helps you make the most of the gifts and opportunities God gives you.

Let's Think About It!

- How can you balance play and work in your daily routine?

- What are some fun activities you can do instead of spending too much time on screens?

- Why is it important to use your time wisely?

Using your time wisely is a skill that will help you succeed and stay happy. By balancing work and play and being mindful of screen time, you can make the most of every day and honor God with your time. You've got this—keep up the great work!

Rule #21: Learn to Say Sorry

Hello! Have you ever done something that hurt someone's feelings or made a mistake you wish you could take back? Saying sorry can be hard, but it's an important way to show you care and want to make things better. Let's learn how to admit when you're wrong and take steps to make things right!

Admit When You're Wrong

We all make mistakes—it's part of being human. Admitting when you're wrong shows that you're honest, humble, and willing to learn from your mistakes.

- **Why Admitting You're Wrong is Important:**

  Pretending you didn't do anything wrong doesn't solve the problem, and it can hurt your relationships. Admitting your mistakes helps others trust you and shows that you're ready to grow.

- **What the Bible Says:**

In Proverbs 28:13, it says:

"Whoever conceals their sins does not prosper, but the one who confesses and renounces them finds mercy."

God is always ready to forgive us when we admit our wrongs and ask for His help.

- **How to Admit You're Wrong:**

  - Take a deep breath and think about what happened.

  - Say, "I'm sorry for what I did," and mean it.

  - Be specific about what you're sorry for, like:

    "I'm sorry I took your toy without asking."

Make Things Right

Saying sorry is the first step, but it's also important to take action to fix what went wrong. Making things right shows that you're truly sorry and want to rebuild trust.

- **Why Making Things Right is Important:**

  Apologies mean more when they're followed by actions. Making things right helps heal hurt feelings and shows that you're serious about doing better.

- **What the Bible Says:**

  In Matthew 5:23-24, Jesus says:

  "Therefore, if you are offering your gift at the altar and there remember that your brother or sister has something against you, leave your gift there in front of the altar. First go and be reconciled to them; then come and offer your gift."

  This reminds us that fixing relationships is important to God.

- **How to Make Things Right:**

  - Ask the person, "What can I do to make it better?"

  - Replace or fix anything you broke or lost.

  - Promise to do better next time and keep your promise.

What Happens When You Say Sorry?

When you say sorry and make things right, you repair relationships and grow stronger as a person. You also feel more peaceful inside because you know you've done the right thing.

- **What the Bible Says:**

In 1 John 1:9, it says:

"If we confess our sins, he is faithful and just and will forgive us our sins and purify us from all unrighteousness."

God forgives us when we say sorry, and He helps us forgive others too.

Let's Think About It!

- Can you think of a time when you said sorry to someone? How did it feel?

- Why is it important to admit when you're wrong, even if it's hard?

- What's one way you can make things right if you've hurt someone's feelings?

Learning to say sorry is a big step toward becoming kind, responsible, and trustworthy. When you admit your mistakes and make things right, you're following God's example of love and forgiveness. Keep practicing—you're doing great!

Conclusion: A Lifetime of Guidance

Congratulations on completing **"Rules Every Child Should Live By."** You have taken an important step in learning how to live a life filled with kindness, wisdom, and faith. These rules were written with love to help guide you as you grow into the amazing person God created you to be.

A Guide to Treasure

This book is more than just a collection of rules—it is a treasure chest of wisdom to help you make the best choices in life. Each rule is like a piece of a puzzle, and when you follow them, they come together to show you the beautiful life God has planned for you.

Remember, these rules are not just for today. They are here to guide you every day of your life. Whenever you feel unsure, lost, or in need of direction, come back to this book. It will remind you of what's right, help you make good decisions, and show you how much God loves you.

What These Rules Mean for You

As you go forward, remember that these rules are here to:

- **Guide Your Actions:** Use them to help you decide how to treat others, how to care for yourself, and how to honor God.

- **Strengthen Your Faith:** Reflect on the Bible verses and lessons in this book to grow closer to God and trust Him in all things.

- **Shape Your Future:** By following these rules, you're building a strong foundation for a bright and successful future.

A Promise from God

The Bible reminds us in Proverbs 3:5-6:

"Trust in the Lord with all your heart and lean not on your own understanding; in all your ways submit to him, and he will make your paths straight."

When you follow these rules and trust God, He will guide you on the right path and bless your life in ways you can't even imagine.

Keep Growing

You are on an incredible journey, and this book is just the beginning. Keep learning, keep growing, and keep trusting God. Every time you follow these rules, you're showing the world the kind, wise, and amazing person you are becoming.

- **Remember to:**

    - Be kind and respectful.

    - Stay curious and open-minded.

    - Take responsibility for your actions.

    - Trust God in everything you do.

A Note to Parents and Guardians

This book is not just for children—it's also a tool for you as parents and guardians. Use it as a guide to teach, correct, and inspire your children. Refer to it when they have questions or need encouragement, and let it be a source of wisdom and love for your family.

Closing Thoughts

Dear child, always remember that God loves you deeply and has a wonderful plan for your life. These rules are here to help you follow that plan and become the best version of yourself. You are special, you are loved, and you are capable of doing great things.

So go out into the world with confidence and kindness, and let these rules guide your steps. You are a light in this world—shine brightly, and make your life a blessing to others!

With love,

Nick Imoru

About the Author

Nick Imoru is a dynamic speaker, author, educator, entrepreneur, and consultant based in Canada. He is the President of Achievers Centre, a division of Philips Reliability Consult Inc. Nick's mission is centered on empowering the human spirit through consulting, coaching, connecting and circulating ideas and information. His goal is to inspire, ignite passion, create profit, and make a spiritual impact, ultimately helping individuals bridge the gap between where they are and where they aspire to be.

Nick holds a B.Eng. in Mechanical and Production Engineering and an MSc. in Advanced Technology from the UK. With over 18 years of experience in the Oil and Gas industry, he specializes in Maintenance & Reliability Engineering and is a Certified Maintenance & Reliability Professional (CMRP), reflecting his commitment to excellence in his field.

As the author of over 20 books and numerous articles and research papers, Nick's work spans personal development, spirituality, academia, business, and finance. He is the founder of Achievers Consult, Achievers Centre, and Achievers Publishing, all operating under Philips Reliability Consult Inc.

Nick is happily married to Dr. Margaret and is a proud father of two daughters, Nelly and Myra. His unwavering dedication to personal and professional growth, combined with his entrepreneurial spirit, continues to make a profound impact on individuals and organizations, guiding them towards success and fulfillment.

With a vision to inspire, train, develop, and unlock potential, Nick Imoru is committed to helping individuals and businesses achieve their highest levels of success.

To contact Nick or learn more about Achievers Centre, opportunities, speeches, and seminars, please use the information below:

Email: Nick@achieverscentre.com
Website: www.achieverscentre.com

Books By Same Author

- A Heart for God
- Operating God's Private Lines
- Growing In Life
- Money & Pleasure: Trap of Purpose
- Success Buttons for Life & Academic Excellence
- The Making of Greatness
- Your Best Year Ever
- Nothing Just Happens
- How Did I Become Like This
- Achievers Daily Tonic
- Living in His Fullness: Unveiling the Life, Mission, Death and Triumph of Jesus
- Your Belief System: How Your Thoughts Dictate Your Life
- The Wit & Wisdom of Dr David Oyedepo
- The Tongue: How Your Words Shape Your Destiny
- He Has Said...So We May Boldly Say
- Character: The Blueprint for a Great Future

- Living in His Light: Understanding Your New Identity in Christ
- Personal & Family Budgeting: Mastering Your Money for Financial Freedom
- Your Money, Your Future: A Student's Guide to Financial Success
- Choosing the Right Path: A Career Guide for Teens and Youth
- Saving Your Future: A Practical Guide to Financial Literacy
- The Power of Your Environment: How Your Surroundings Shape Your Life
- Think It, Do It: How to Turn Thoughts into Meaningful Action
- Adventures in God's Amazing Storybook, Part 1
- Adventures in God's Amazing Storybook, Part 2

To order any of these books, please visit:

Our online shop @ www.achieverscentre.com

or any of the amazon websites:

www.amazon.ca

www.amazon.com

www.amazon.co.uk, etc